The Berenstain Bears' SCIENCE and NATURE SUPER TREASURY

BOOK ONE
The Berenstain Bears' ALMANAC

BOOK TWO
The Berenstain Bears' NATURE GUIDE

BOOK THREE
The Berenstain Bears' SCIENCE FAIR

Bear Facts Library™

The Berenstain Bears' ALMANAC

A Year in Bear Country...

holidays

seasons

weather

actual facts about snow, wind, rain, thunder, lightning, the sun, the moon...

and

lots

more

by Stan and Jan Berenstain

Random House · New York

First paperback edition 1984. Copyright © 1973 by Berenstains, Inc. All rights reserved under International and Pan-American Copyright Conventions. Published in the United States by Random House, Inc., New York, and simultaneously in Canada by Random House of Canada Limited, Toronto. *Library of Congress Cataloging in Publication Data:* Berenstain, Stanley. The bears' almanac. SUMMARY: The further adventures of the Bear family also include information on holidays, weather, and the seasons. [1. Bears—Stories. 2. Seasons—Fiction. 3. Stories in rhyme] I. Berenstain, Janice, joint author. II. Title. PZ7.B4483Baf [Fic] 73-2298 ISBN: 0-394-82693-0 (trade hardcover); 0-394-92693-5 (library binding); 0-394-86601-0 (trade paperback)   Manufactured in the United States of America 14 15 16 17

The Berenstain Bears'
ALMANAC

A Year in Bear Country

What makes a year?

Four Seasons. Four is all.
Winter, Spring, Summer, Fall.

Twelve Months. A lot to say.
January, February,
March, April, May.
June, July,
August, September.
October, November
and December.

How will you know
which season is here?
Come and we'll show you
a Bear Country year.

A brand-new calendar!
Hooray! Hooray!
A whole new year
starts today!

In the very first month
on the very first day . . .

HAPPY NEW YEAR!

is what we say.

The first three months of the year are WINTER

JANUARY
FEBRUARY
MARCH

HOW WILL YOU KNOW IT'S WINTER?

Your knees shiver.

You see ice on the river.

Your breath shows.

You've got a
runny nose.

You have to wear a scarf and cap.

Great Natural Bear
starts his
LONG winter nap.

Good night, Small Bear.

See you next Spring.

GREAT
NATURAL
BEAR'S
LAIR

Papa puts on long underwear.

There are
fat snowflakes in the air.

11

The red in the thermometer
starts to fall.
Sometimes there's hardly any
red at all.

Brrr!
IT'S WINTER!

When it's cold
the clouds freeze.
Clouds turn into flakes of ice.
The ice flakes fall . . .
That's **snow**.
Children think it's nice.

ACTUAL
FACTUAL
BEAR

Some places have no snow,
you'll find.
Children there
don't seem to mind.

In sunny places
such as these,
it's just too hot
for clouds to freeze.

13

Sometimes snow
comes and goes in a hurry.

When snow does that . . .

it's called a **flurry.**

A blizzard . . .

That is what we call
a really, really
BIG snowfall.

You may see it flurry.
You may see it fly ...
But there's more to snow
than meets the eye.

You are different
from your sisters and brothers.

And EVERY snowflake
is different from the others.

That is a very nice
thing to know
the next time you are
watching snow.

sick in bed

nose drops

brand-new sled

belly flops

spinning wheels

snowmobiles

He can skate
a figure eight.

Say! Look what
she can do . . .
six thousand
nine hundred
thirty-two!

tow truck

stick

puck

goalie

goal

barrel jump

ker-thump!

In February, on **Valentine's Day**...

I LOVE YOU IS WHAT WE SAY

FEBRUARY
14
VALENTINE'S DAY

I Love You

20

But . . . if you're shy . . .
GUESS WHO
will do.

GUESS
WHO!

In
MARCH,
friends,
Winter
ends.

21

The next three months of the year are SPRING

| APRIL | MAY | JUNE |

HOW WILL YOU KNOW IT'S SPRING?

There is slush and mush from melting snow.

Birds sing.
Plants grow.

A crocus grows right through the snow.

Wind blows hats off people's heads.

We take out bikes.
We put back sleds.

I't's time to get out
brooms and mops.

I't starts to rain . . .

then it stops.

The sun begins
to warm the air.

Nice
day,
Small Bear.

Great Natural Bear
comes out
of his lair . . .

Hooray!
IT'S SPRING!

The first day in April
is **APRIL FOOL'S DAY.**

Your friends will try
to fool you today.
Here are some of the
things they will say . . .

There's a bug
on your nose!

Your shoes
are not tied!

There's a hole
in your pants!

There's a big purple
monster outside!!

Of course there isn't
a bug
on your nose.

There's no hole
in your pants.

And your shoes
are both tied.

And as for big purple monsters . . .

Help! A big purple
monster is waiting
outside!

FLYING A KITE . . .

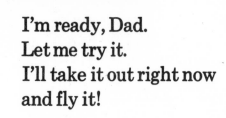

Is a very fine thing
that you and I
can do in Spring .

I'm ready, Dad.
Let me try it.
I'll take it out right now
and fly it!

Not yet, my boy.
Hold on, Son.
First I'll show you
how it's done.

Now, check the string.
You need a lot.
You also need
a windy spot.

But, Papa!
For a kite to sail . . .
doesn't it have
to have a tail?

Yes, Small Bear.
You are learning how.
This nice long tail
goes on right now!

Next, you must know
which way to run.
Watch the wind blow
and go that way, Son.

But, Dad!
Is that way right?
Shouldn't you run
the other way
with a kite?

Right! Here we go!
Hold the kite high!
I'll let out some string
and we'll let 'er fly!

I get it, Dad! ...
Except for one thing.
Didn't you let out
too much string?

31

Son, I showed you
how to do it right.
Now why don't you just
go fly your kite?

What you
will need.

A good strong kite.
Plenty of string.
A nice long tail.
A day in Spring.

ACTUAL FACTS ABOUT WIND

Air. Air.
It's everywhere.
When it moves

from here . . .

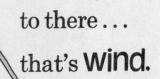

to there . . .
that's **wind**.

The wind sails boats . . .

and paper planes.

It turns windmills . . .

and weather vanes.

A weather vane always shows
just which way the wind blows.

A soft, soft wind
blows the trees ....
A soft, soft wind
is called a **breeze**.

But ...
Sometimes the wind
is so strong that
it blows off
Farmer Ben Bear's hat.

It blows away
his stool and pail ....
THAT kind of wind
is called a **gale**.

A tornado.

A tornado!

That's when
the big wind lifts
poor Farmer Ben.
It lifts him, cow and all,
and then . . .
It whirls him round
and round again.

It's kind of hard
on Farmer Ben.

ACTUAL FACTS ABOUT RAIN

There are drops of water
in the clouds.
They are very, very small.
When they get together,
they get big enough
to fall.
That's **rain**.

When just a few
drops fall,
a **drizzle** is what you get.
A drizzle isn't much . . . .
You don't get very wet.

When more
drops fall,
a **shower**
is what you get.
A shower makes you
very wet.

When millions of drops
pour down
a **downpour** is what you get.

A downpour
makes you
SOAKING
wet.

After the rain,
sometimes
a **rainbow** is what you get.

A rainbow is worth
all that wet.

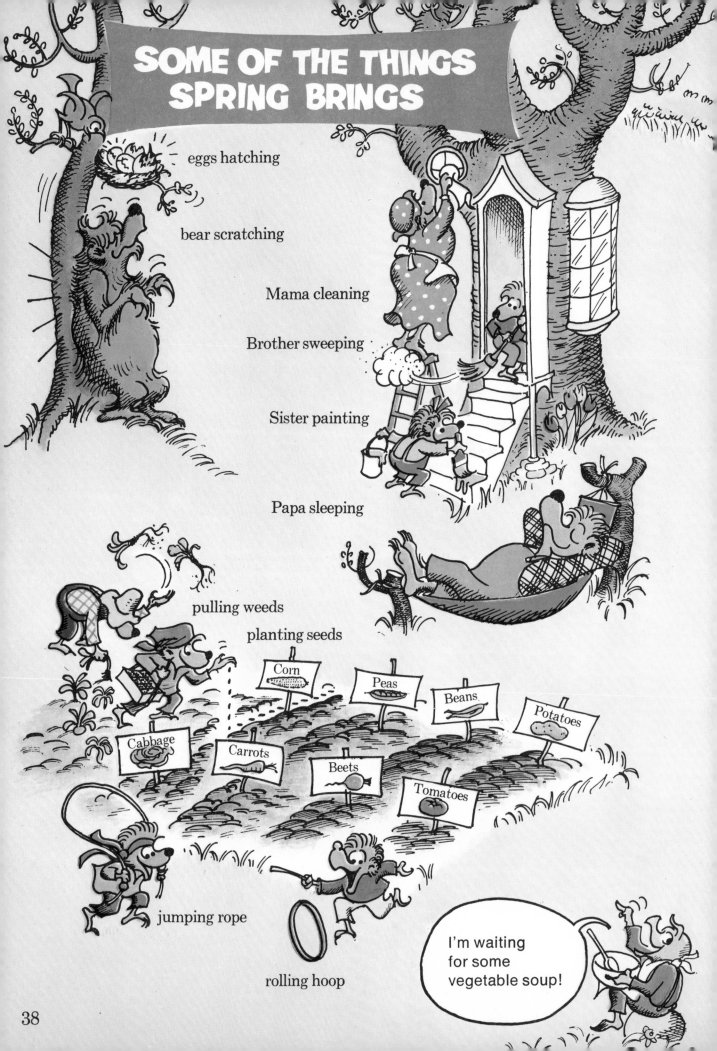

SOME OF THE THINGS SPRING BRINGS

eggs hatching

bear scratching

Mama cleaning

Brother sweeping

Sister painting

Papa sleeping

pulling weeds

planting seeds

Corn

Peas

Beans

Potatoes

Cabbage

Carrots

Beets

Tomatoes

jumping rope

rolling hoop

I'm waiting for some vegetable soup!

The next three months of the year are

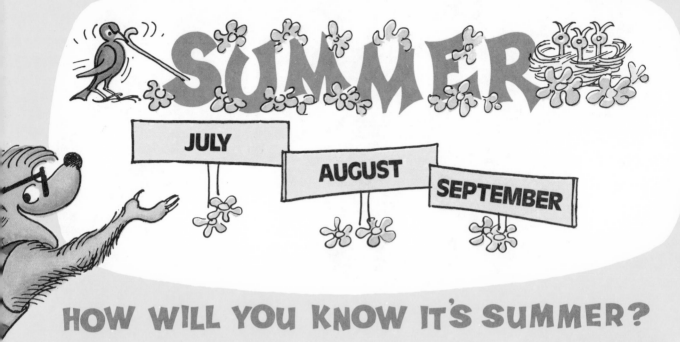

SUMMER

JULY

AUGUST

SEPTEMBER

HOW WILL YOU KNOW IT'S SUMMER?

There's no more school.

CLOSED FOR SUMMER

Papa's in the swimming pool.

Mama's making
lemonade.

Granny's sitting
in the shade.

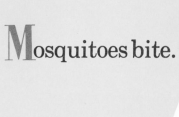

Mosquitoes bite.

You go to bed when
it's still light.

E verybody's very lazy . . .

except for plants.

They grow like crazy.

T he red in the
thermometer
shoots up tall.
There's hardly any
room at all.

Phew!
IT'S SUMMER!

ACTUAL FACTS ABOUT THE SUN

The sun
is millions
of miles away.
But it works for us
every day.

Farmer Ben's plants
need light and heat
to grow into things
we like to eat.

Sun makes wheat
and corn grow tall.

Without it,
they would not grow
at all.

There would be

no peas . . .

or beans . . .

. . . or tomatoes.

We wouldn't even
have potatoes.

The sun helps potatoes
grow fat and round . . .
even though
they're
underground.

The sun can turn
a seed this small
into a sunflower
ten feet tall!

45

The sun warms ponds
where fish eggs hatch.

And gives me lots
of fish to catch.

The sun warms turtles.
It warms frogs.

We love to lie
on sunny logs.

Bats and owls
stay out of it.

We don't like the sun
one bit.

It's good for lying in hammocks . . . .

And splashing under hoses . . . .

But don't stay out in the sun too long . . .

Too much is bad for noses.

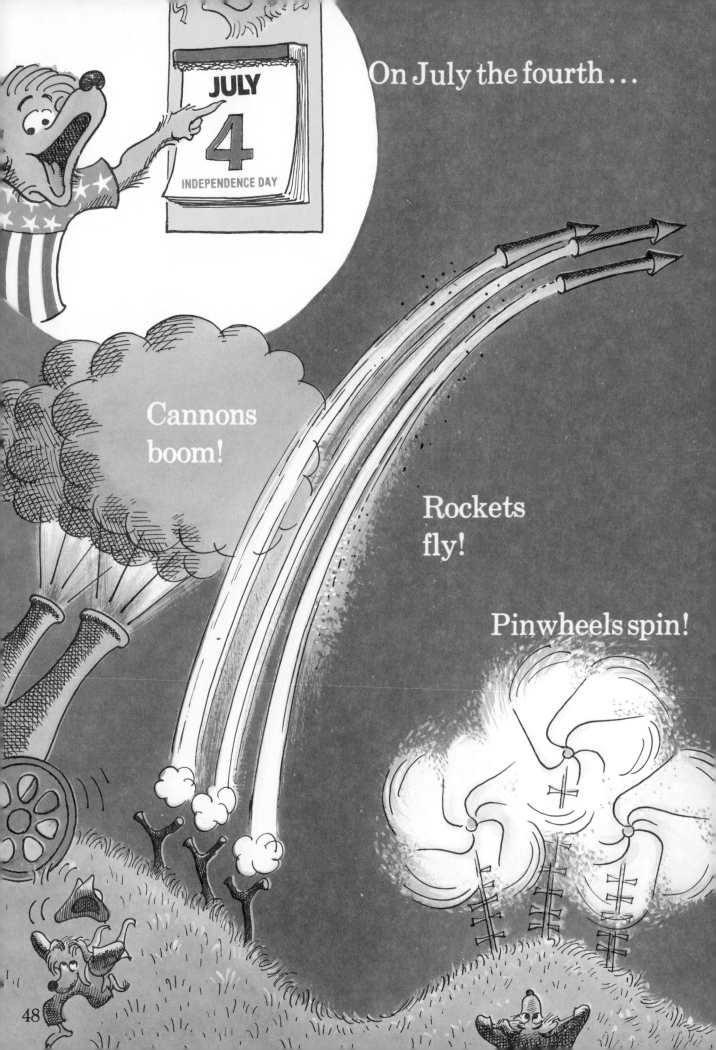

Fireworks fill the sky!

Why?

Because July the fourth
is **THE FOURTH OF JULY**

It is also known as

INDEPENDENCE DAY

And on this day, we all say...

HAPPY BIRTHDAY USA

SUMMER BRINGS SUN AND FUN

swimming

floating

diving

boating

tanning

fanning

A bite!
Look!

No hook!

outdoor cook

ACTUAL FACTS ABOUT THUNDER AND LIGHTNING

Electricity
in your home
lights your lights.
It runs
the vacuum
for your mother.

Electricity
in the clouds
shoots
giant sparks
from one cloud
to another.

That's lightning.

Sometimes it's
pretty frightening.

When lightning flashes
from cloud to cloud,
it makes a noise
that's VERY loud.

If you wonder . . .
That's thunder.

KA-BOOOM

Something
to remember:
Summer ends
in September.

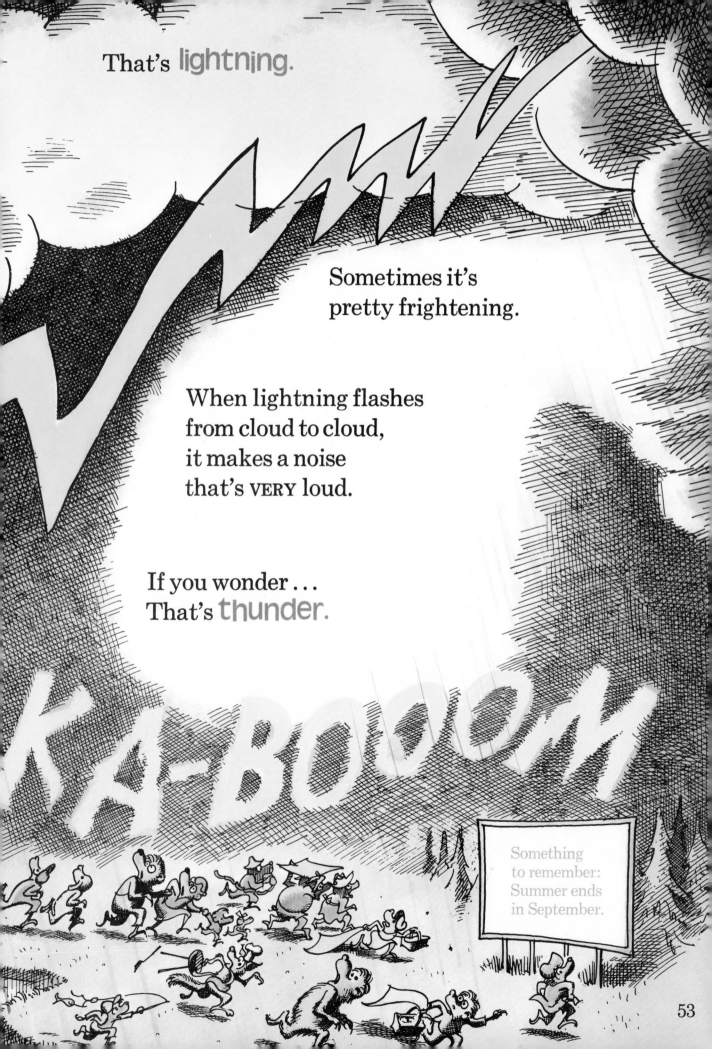

53

The next three months of the year are FALL

OCTOBER

NOVEMBER

DECEMBER

HOW WILL YOU KNOW IT'S FALL?

This is the time
of the Harvest Moon ...

The time when the
caterpillar
makes his cocoon.

54

The weather
turns a little cool.

Some of us
are back in school.

Birds flying south
fill the sky.

Summer plants
turn brown and dry.

There are lots
of pumpkins
and apples around.

There is a red and gold
carpet of leaves
on the ground.

So it must be
FALL!

57

October ends with **Halloween**...
Time for trick-or-treat.
We go out in funny clothes
and get good things to eat.

witch

clown

knight-in-armor

pirate

devil

pumpkin

farmer

ghost

skeleton

big black cat

monster

Help!
A giant bat!

58

When is **Thanksgiving?**
Here's how to remember.
It's the fourth Thursday
That comes in November.

NOVEMBER

THANKSGIVING

turkey

stuffing

gravy

yams

rolls

butter

jellies

jams

corn

honey

hot mince pie

fruits

nuts

pumpkin pie

Father

Mother

Sister

Brother

... All are thankful for each other.

ACTUAL FACTS ABOUT
THE MOON

FULL MOON

Sometimes the moon
is round and bright.
It lights the way
for us at night.

CRESCENT MOON

On other nights
the moon is slim.
There is light.
But the light is dim.

NO MOON

It gets very, very dark
when there is no moon in sight.

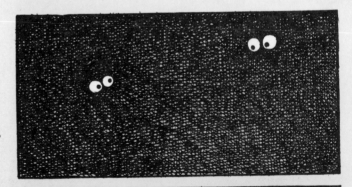

If you go out
on nights like these,
be sure to take a light.

The moon looks like
a smooth round ball.
But a close look will show you
the moon's not smooth at all.

Some day soon,
you may go
to the moon.
You'll wave good-bye
to your father and mother....

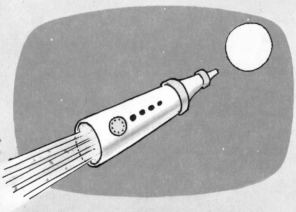

You'll rocket to the moon ...

and get a moon rock
for your brother.

In December,
friends,
Fall ends.

DECEMBER
25
CHRISTMAS DAY

December is the last
month of the year
and the very best day
of all is here!

star

tinsel

candy cane

light

ball

bell

chain

Santa's reindeer

electric train

doll

truck

Jack-in-the-box

boat   jet

building blocks

mittens

hat

pair of socks

cookies

fruit cake

candy bar

puzzle

book

wind-up car

stockings

sled

HONEY

honey jar

On this day...

MERRY CHRISTMAS

is what we say!

ACTUAL FACTUAL BEAR

63

It's New Year's Eve!
A whole year ends.

Tomorrow we'll
start
a NEW YEAR,
friends.

So, now, we can
all turn back
to the beginning
of our Almanac.

The Berenstain Bears' SCIENCE and NATURE Super Treasury

BOOK ONE
The Berenstain Bears'
ALMANAC

BOOK TWO
The Berenstain Bears'
NATURE GUIDE

BOOK THREE
The Berenstain Bears'
SCIENCE FAIR

Bear Facts Library™

ACTUAL
FACTUAL
BEAR

The Berenstain Bears' NATURE GUIDE

Almost everything small bears and kids need to know about...

the animals

the plants

the earth itself

ACTUAL FACTUAL BEAR

GREAT NATURE

with actual facts about frogs, possums, birds, fish, trees, rocks, ladybugs, earthquakes...

and lots more

by Stan and Jan Berenstain

Random House · New York

First paperback edition 1984. Copyright © 1975 by Berenstains, Inc. All rights reserved under International and Pan-American Copyright Conventions. Published in the United States by Random House, Inc., New York, and simultaneously in Canada by Random House of Canada Limited, Toronto. *Library of Congress Cataloging in Publication Data:* Berenstain, Stanley. The bears' nature guide. SUMMARY: On a nature walk Papa Bear introduces animals, plants, and other beauties and wonders of the earth. 1. Nature—Juvenile literature. [1. Nature] I. Berenstain, Janice, joint author. II. Title. QH48.B46 500.9 75-8070 ISBN: 0-394-83125-X (trade hardcover); 0-394-93125-4 (library binding); 0-394-86602-9 (trade paperback)   Manufactured in the United States of America 1 2 3 4 5 6 7 8 9 0

Come!
The wonders of nature
await you outside
with me, Papa Bear,
as your nature walk guide.

In all my years
as a nature guide
I have followed one rule
far and wide:
Be alert for any
sign or sound—
the wonders of nature
are all around!

4

YIPE!

Now THERE'S a wonder of nature
not many have seen.

Wow! Papa Bear!
We see what you mean!

ACTUAL FACTS ABOUT NATURE

WHAT IS NATURE?

It's everybody
and everything—

a peacock's tail,

a butterfly's wing.

It's snails

and stones

and dinosaur bones.

Volcanoes!

Earthquakes . . .

Cousin Liz!

That's just a PART

of what nature is.

Nature is
THE WORLD OF ANIMALS—

from the biggest whale . . .

to the smallest flea.

IT'S THE WORLD OF PLANTS—

from the tiniest weed . . .

to the tallest tree.

IT'S THE EARTH ITSELF—

the rocks . . .
and soil.

And from under the earth

come coal and oil.

9

13

16

ARE YOU AN ANIMAL?

1. Animals are living things

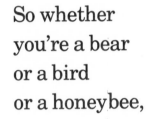

So whether
you're a bear
or a bird
or a honeybee,

if you're ALIVE,
you just might be—

an ANIMAL.

2. Animals can move around

They can walk or run,

fly or glide,

swim,

jump, crawl,

or slide.

Plants can't
move around.
They are rooted
to the ground.

So,
if you're ALIVE
and MOVE AROUND
and are not rooted
to the ground,
then it seems,
at least so far,
an animal
is what you are.

ACTUAL
FACTUAL
BEAR

18

A few animals ARE
rooted to the ground.

The sponge is one.
To be a sponge
is not much fun.

3. Animals need food to stay alive

If PLANTS are what
you like to eat,
the word for you
is **herbivore**.

If MEAT is what
you like to eat,
the word for you
is **carnivore**.

Great Natural Bear
eats either/or.
The word for him
is **omnivore**.

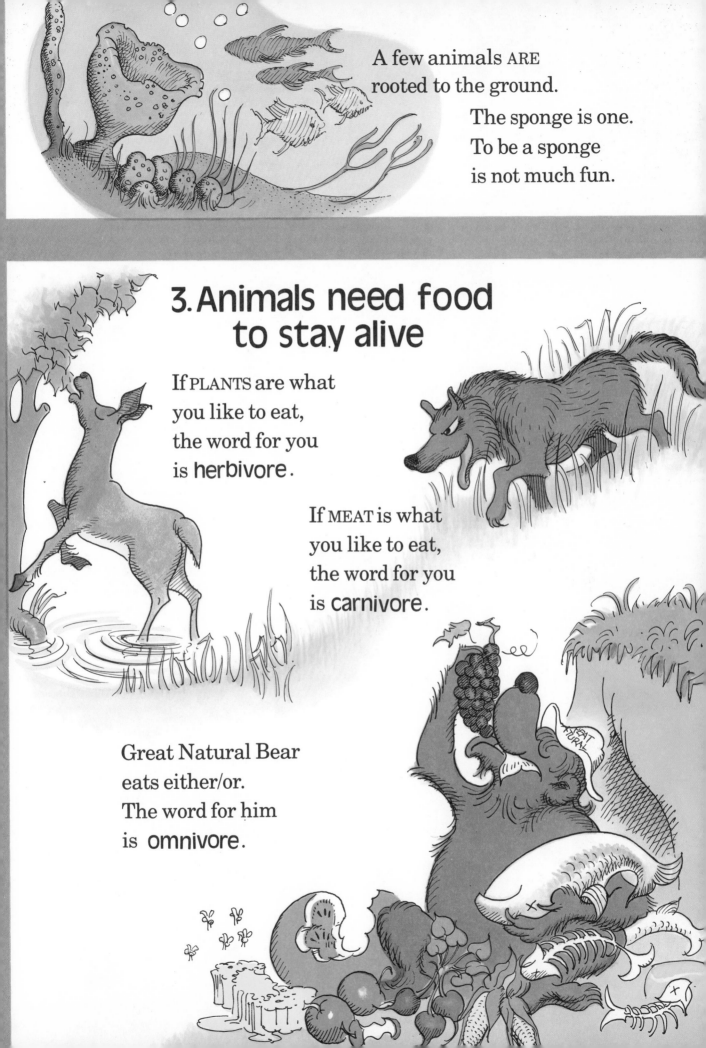

So-o-o,
if you're ALIVE
and MOVE AROUND,
if you NEED FOOD
to survive,
it's beginning
more and more
to seem
that you can join
the animal team!

4. Animals reproduce

A good thing, too!
If they didn't,
there wouldn't be
a me or you.

They reproduce
in different ways.

We hatch from eggs
our mother lays!

Sister Bear
and her brother
grew from eggs
inside their mother.

Some animals are
so very small
they do not come
from eggs at all.

What do these tiny creatures do?

They grow until . . .   they split in two.

So-o-o-o,
if you're ALIVE
and MOVE AROUND,
if you NEED FOOD
and REPRODUCE,
then—
whether you are
mite or moose,
bee, baboon,
or silly goose—
I'm sure that
you can plainly see
an animal IS
what you must be!

22

THE BEAUTIES OF NATURE ARE ALL AROUND...

As your nature walk guide
I have many duties.
Now let's take a moment
to enjoy nature's beauties.

Feel the hush
of a woodland glade,

the sudden cool
of woodland shade.

After the sunlight
it's hard to see

the moss . . . the vines . . .

the twisty old tree

all reflected
in a woodland pool.

24

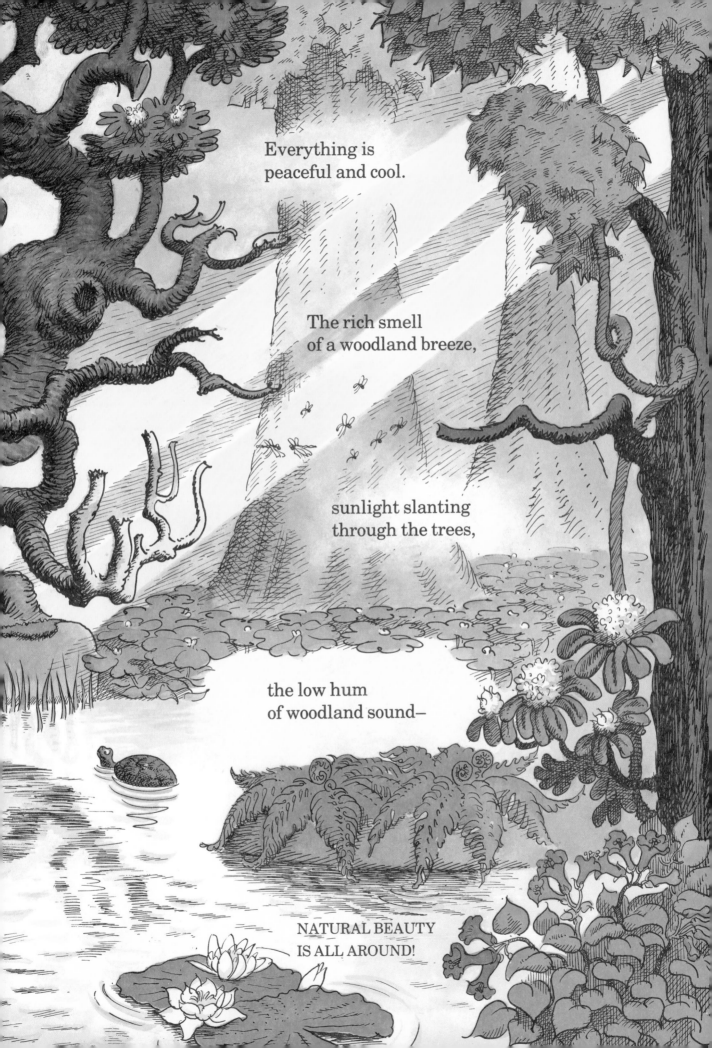

Everything is peaceful and cool.

The rich smell of a woodland breeze,

sunlight slanting through the trees,

the low hum of woodland sound—

NATURAL BEAUTY IS ALL AROUND!

MAMMALS

These are all animals
that we call MAMMALS.

Mammals grow
fur or hair.

Some have a lot,
like Great Natural Bear.

Others — just a little,
scattered here and there.

Mammals have their babies live.
That is, MOTHER mammals do.

Some of them
have a lot.

Others — one or two.

27

Mammals nurse their young.
That is, MOTHER mammals do.

This works very well
when feeding one or two.

But if, like Mother Possum,
you have many mouths to feed,
you are going to have
a busy time indeed.

Porpoises and whales—
they are mammals, too.
They nurse their babies
in the sea—
not an easy thing to do.

There are
many strange
and odd-shaped
mammals,
like walruses
and two-humped camels.

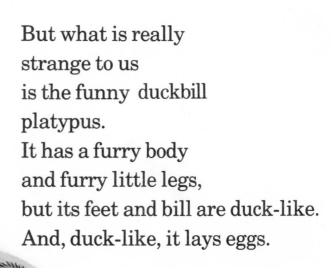

But what is really
strange to us
is the funny duckbill
platypus.
It has a furry body
and furry little legs,
but its feet and bill are duck-like.
And, duck-like, it lays eggs.

THE BEARS' OFFICIAL BIRD WATCHING STATION

THE BIRDS' OFFICIAL BEAR WATCHING STATION

Birds come
in many colors
and have many
different habits.

Robin Redbreast
catches worms.

Owls catch mice
and rabbits.

Papa Cardinal
is very red.

Mama's mostly brown.

The white-breasted nuthatch
has dinner upside-down.

The vulture sees
for miles around.

Canada goose
makes a honking sound.

Hermit thrush is very shy.

Hawk is fierce and bold.

Stormy petrel likes the rain.

Junco likes the cold.

Some birds are
very proud.
They say their names
right out loud.

Towhee says, "Towhee! Towhee!"

Chickadee says, "Chickadee-dee-dee!"

Guess who says "Bob White! Bob White!"

If you guessed bobwhite,
you're right!

Oriole's nest
is one of the best.
It's big and strong
and round.

Killdeer builds
no nest at all.
It lays its eggs
on the ground!

31

Cowbirds are not
very good mothers.
They lay their eggs
in the nests of others.

See the great
brown pelican.
Its bill holds more
than its belly can.

Ducks and geese
are waterfowl.

ADVICE TO
MICE:
Beware of
owl!

Seagulls like
to swoop and soar.

Sandpipers run
along the shore.

The martin likes
apartment houses.

A wren's front door
is the size of a mouse's.

Mockingbird can imitate
the robin when it sings.

When looking for a mate
the ruffed grouse drums its wings.

The ostrich stands
eight feet tall.
For its size
its wings are small.
Maybe that's
the reason why
the mighty ostrich
cannot fly.

What about the kiwi?
Why can't the kiwi fly?
If you ever saw one,
you wouldn't wonder why!

On any nature
walk I take,
I always go past
Great Swamp Lake.

Turtles! Lizards!
A water snake!
REPTILES live in
Great Swamp Lake!

If we wait
a little while,
we might even see
a crocodile.

I already
see one, Dad.

You're standing on him—
AND HE LOOKS MAD!

Reptiles such as
lizard, snake, and crocodile
have been on earth
a long, long while.

Their cousin,
mighty dinosaur,
doesn't live here
anymore.

Extinct's the word
for dinosaur.

Dinosaur

35

Here's the story
of a toad and a frog,
two AMPHIBIANS
from Swampuddle Bog:

One afternoon
a toad and a frog
were napping together
in Swampuddle Bog.

A fine, fat fly
came a-buzzin'
right between
the toad and his cousin.

The toad and the frog
each opened an eye
and thought to themselves,
"A fine, fat fly!

ACTUAL FACTS
ABOUT
TOADS & FROGS

First, the mother
lays her eggs.

Tads hatch out.

The tads grow legs.

36

"I'll shoot out my tongue
with a zip and a zap,
have a quick swallow,
and go on with my nap."

Out came the tongues
as quick as a shot
and tied themselves up
in a big sticky knot.

Where was the fly?
The fly was still there,
but the two sticky tongues
were stuck in midair!

To untangle them took
the rest of the day
and as for the fly
. . . he got away.

And what do we learn
from that fly that came buzzin'?
Never stick out
your tongue at your cousin!

They grow until   **one fine day**   **they lose their tails**   **and hop away!** 37

FISH
AND OTHER
ANIMALS OF THE SEA

Another kind of animal can easily be seen from Actual Factual's submarine!

sardine

bass

tuna

flounder

That sunfish is a thousand-pounder!

sawfish

sailfish

swordfish

codfish

Sea horse is the ocean's odd fish!

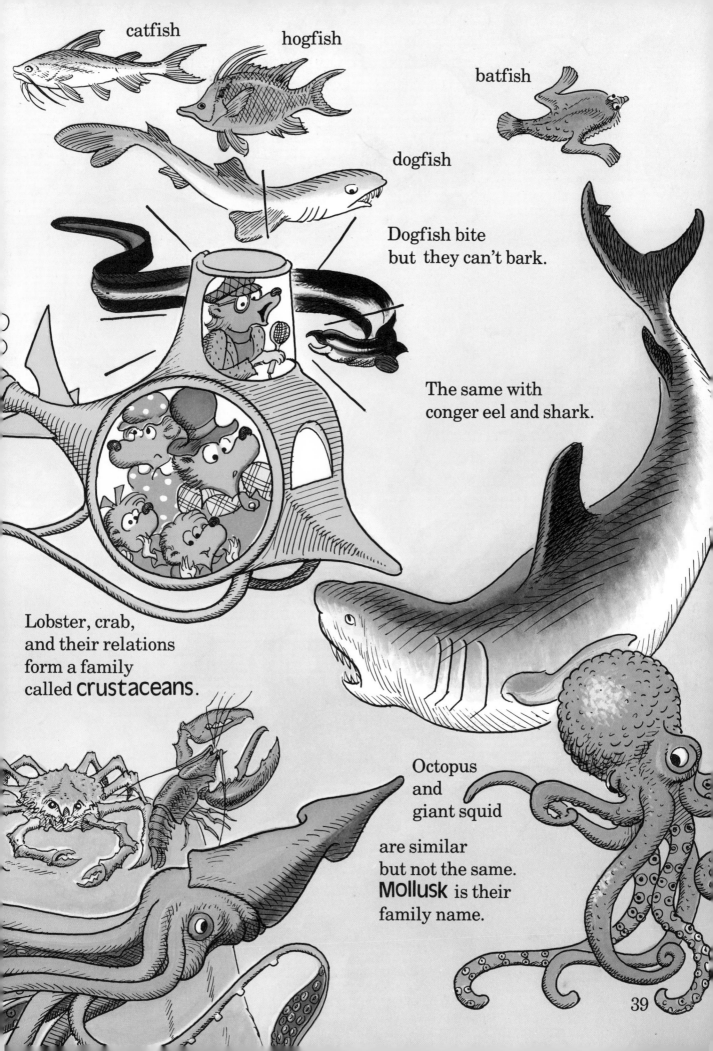

catfish

hogfish

batfish

dogfish

Dogfish bite
but they can't bark.

The same with
conger eel and shark.

Lobster, crab,
and their relations
form a family
called crustaceans.

Octopus
and
giant squid

are similar
but not the same.
Mollusk is their
family name.

39

41

ACTUAL FACTS ABOUT THE WORLD OF PLANTS

WHAT A PLANT CAN DO AND WHAT IT CAN'T

You can visit your friends and watch TV.

A plant can't.

You can jump a puddle and climb a tree.

A plant can't.

You can also
read and write.

A plant can't even
fly a kite.

But there are things
plants CAN do
that you and I
could NEVER do!

When water rushes
through your yard
in very rainy weather,
all the grass roots
underground
hold the soil together.

In places where
you have no lawn
you may find
the soil is gone!

Plants are
food for us to eat—

every cabbage,
bean, and beet,
all the rice
and corn
and wheat.

And, in a way,
plants help make meat.

Look at chickens—

THEY feed
on grain and seed.

Plants are also
very good
at making different
kinds of wood.

The wood for houses,
boats, and skis

comes from different
kinds of trees.

Even clothes
can come from plants,
like jeans
and cotton underpants.

COTTON PLANT

GREEN NAT

Plants help make the air we breathe.
They make a gas called **oxygen**,
the gas we use
when breathing IN.

Plants need a gas
called CO_2,
which they get
from me and you.
WE breathe OUT CO_2.

That's something
we can think about
as we are breathing
in and out.

So, next time
you meet a plant,
remember . . .
what a plant CAN do
is more important
than what it can't.

47

ACTUAL FACTS ABOUT
THE DIFFERENT KINDS OF PLANTS

The biggest, strongest
plant we see
is the kind of plant
we call a tree.

Elm is smooth.

Hickory's rough.

Willow bends.

Oak is tough!

Pine and spruce
are **evergreens**.
They keep their leaves
year round.

The **broad-leafs**
lose theirs in the fall.
You'll find them
lying on the ground.

No matter how many
kinds you name,
in some ways trees
are all the same.

Their roots grow deep
into the ground.
Their trunks of wood
grow thick and round.

Trees are covered
with a skin called bark.
See for yourself
in a woods or a park.

49

Flowering plants
are pretty.
Many smell good, too.
But flowers
aren't just pretty—
they have a job to do.
In all such plants,
even WEEDS,
the flower's job
is making seeds.

ESPECIALLY weeds!

Most kinds of plants need water
almost every day.
But not the kind called cactus—
it's built a different way.
Cactus stores up water
in its special stem.
When animals try to get it . . .
OUCH! Too bad for them!

Algae forms
thick green scum.

Great Natural tried
to walk on some.

The green
one often sees
on the shady side of trees
is **moss**.

If you study **ferns** you will find

they don't just grow,

they UNWIND!

When an orange
gets all yucky
because it's very old,
a plant is growing on it.
That yucky plant
is **mold**.

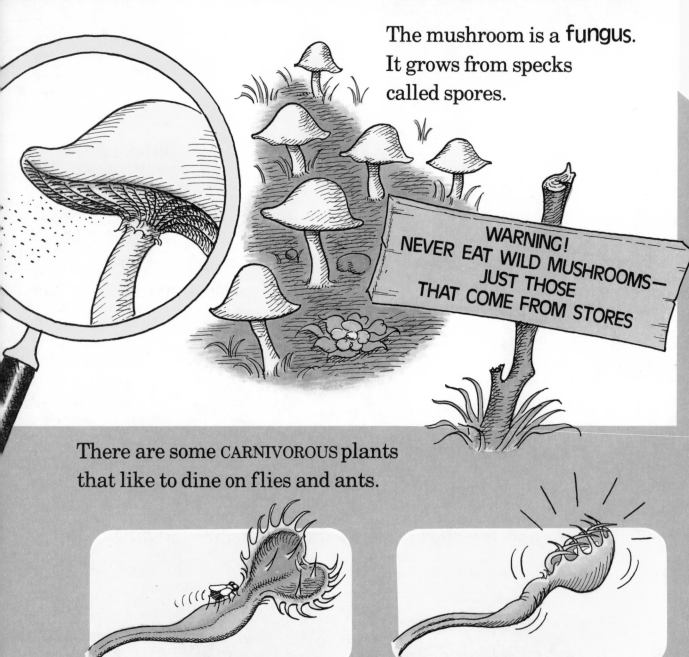

The mushroom is a **fungus**.
It grows from specks
called spores.

WARNING!
NEVER EAT WILD MUSHROOMS—
JUST THOSE
THAT COME FROM STORES

There are some CARNIVOROUS plants
that like to dine on flies and ants.

Like the Venus's-flytrap . . .

CRUNCH!
It just had a fly for lunch.

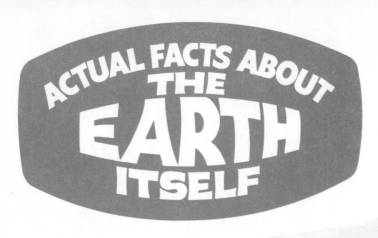

Water helps
to shape the land.

The ocean brings
the shore its sand.

But during storms,
the ocean may
wash some sandy
beach away.

Rivers help
to shape the land.

A river made
Grand Canyon grand!

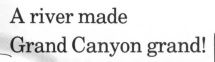

Freezing water
does its part, too.

Ice can crack
a rock in two.

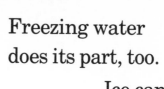

With the right
amount of rain,
this flat land
we call a **plain**
is a perfect place
for growing grain.

If you take away
the rain supply,
you get a **desert**
brown and dry.

55

As we cross the land
we can see
how different
its shapes can be.

This high ground
is called a hill.

A mountain's
even higher still.

Tall mountains
may be snow-capped.

Others may wear green.

Valley is
the name we give
the low place
in between.

Hollow places
are called **caves**.

In the ones
deep underground

Stalactites
and
Stalagmites

are very
often found.

Water dripping
in the caves
is the reason
they have grown,
because, you see,
each water drop
carries bits of stone.

And even though
inside some caves
it's always drippy weather,

it takes

about

a million

years

for them

to grow   together.

A Reminder:
Stalactite and stalagmite—
only caves have got 'em.
Tite is always on the top
and mite is on the bottom.

lake

falls

rapids

creek

cliff

ledge

snow-capped peak

Beyond the earth,
the setting sun.
Our nature walk
is almost done.

Now you know some things
you didn't know before.
Next time you study nature
you'll learn a few things more.

64

The Berenstain Bears'
SCIENCE and NATURE
Super Treasury

BOOK ONE
The Berenstain Bears'
ALMANAC

BOOK TWO
The Berenstain Bears'
NATURE GUIDE

BOOK THREE
The Berenstain Bears'
SCIENCE FAIR

Bear Facts Library™

The Berenstain Bears'
SCIENCE FAIR

The Berenstain Bears' SCIENCE FAIR

ACTUAL FACTUAL BEAR

MACHINES AND HOW THEY WORK

THE SCIENCE OF **MATTER**

ACTUAL FACTS ABOUT **ENERGY**

PROJECTS and **EXPERIMENTS**

THINGS TO MAKE AND DO . . .

and lots more!

by Stan and Jan Berenstain

The bears are going to have a science fair.
Small Bear and Sister want to make something
for the fair. This is a good time for Papa
to give them some science lessons.

First paperback edition 1984. Copyright © 1977 by Berenstains, Inc. All rights reserved under International and Pan-American Copyright Conventions. Published in the United States by Random House, Inc., New York, and simultaneously in Canada by Random House of Canada Limited, Toronto. *Library of Congress Cataloging in Publication Data:* Berenstain, Stanley. The Berenstain Bears' science fair. SUMMARY: Papa Bear teaches Small Bear and Sister about machines, matter, and energy, and helps them prepare projects for science fair. 1. Science—Juvenile literature. 2. Science—Exhibitions—Juvenile literature. [1. Science] I. Berenstain, Janice, joint author. II. Title. Q163.B498   500   76-8121   ISBN: 0-394-83294-9 (trade hardcover); 0-394-93294-3 (library binding); 0-394-86608-7 (trade paperback) Manufactured in the United States of America   1 2 3 4 5 6 7 8 9 0

To make a good project
for the Bears' Science Fair,
you must learn about science.
Follow me, Sister! Come along, Small Bear!

As an old science student
I know just where to start . . .

It's lucky for us, Dad,
that you are so smart!

DANGER
MACHINES
AT
WORK

6

To teach science well,
to make science fun,
I start with *machines*! ...
Put on a safety hat, Son!

DANGER
MACHINES
AT
WORK

And here's your first lesson—
Be very careful near a machine!

Right, Papa Bear.
We see what you mean.

THREE SIMPLE MACHINES

Now the three most important
machines, I feel,
are the simple lever,
the wedge and the wheel.

GREAT
NATURAL
BEAR'S
LAIR

1. THE LEVER

← Press down here

to lift up here. ↖

WHEN A POLE OR
BAR IS USED TO LIFT
OR PRY, IT BECOMES
A LEVER.

ACTUAL
ACTUAL
BEAR

Ahem! . . .

11

I like to make posters.
Here's how I do it—

See this big piece of cardboard
with pictures stuck to it?

LEVERS

A
SCIENCE FAIR POSTER
by Sister Bear

WE USE LEVERS
IN MANY WAYS—

TO OPEN CANS...

JARS...

AND BOTTLES...

jack

TO LIFT CARS...

TO STOP CARS...

brake

TO PUMP WATER.

The lever lifts up here.

You push down here.

Water comes out here.

12

SOMETIMES WE USE
TWO LEVERS TOGETHER—

TO CRACK NUTS...

TO CLIP TOENAILS...

TO SQUEEZE
ORANGES.

MANY TOOLS ARE LEVERS—

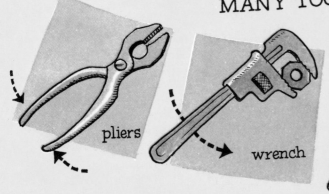

pliers

wrench

hammer

We use levers every day.
They make hard jobs easier
and they let us do things we're
not strong enough to do ourselves.

13

2. THE WEDGE

Push down here...

to split or spread log here.

THE WEDGE IS USED TO SPLIT THINGS OR TO SPREAD THINGS APART.

The **wedge** has many uses.
Splitting logs is one.
Our friendly neighbor, Farmer Ben,
will show us how it's done.

WOK !

Thank you, Ben.
As I said before,
that's one of its uses.
It has many more!

OTHER WAYS WE USE THE WEDGE

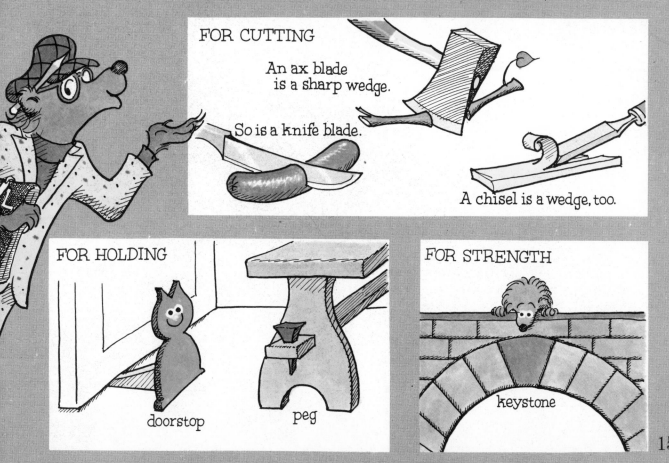

FOR CUTTING

An ax blade
is a sharp wedge.

So is a knife blade.

A chisel is a wedge, too.

FOR HOLDING

doorstop

peg

FOR STRENGTH

keystone

15

Now here is a tool
that's both lever <u>and</u> wedge!

scythe

The handle's a lever.
The blade is a wedge.

It cuts weeds fast
with a stroke that's neat.

That certainly was
both fast and neat.
But you didn't cut weeds.
You cut Farmer Ben's wheat!

16

A simple machine
we use a good deal
is our greatest invention.
It's called THE WHEEL!

3. THE WHEEL

Turn this way...   to go this way.

axle

A WHEEL IS ROUND.
IT TURNS AROUND
A ROD CALLED AN AXLE
THAT RUNS THROUGH
THE CENTER.

Here we have wheels of every kind.
Let's see how many we can find.

wagon wheel

auto wheel

truck wheel

train wheel

water wheel

paddle wheel

ship's wheel

plane wheel

18

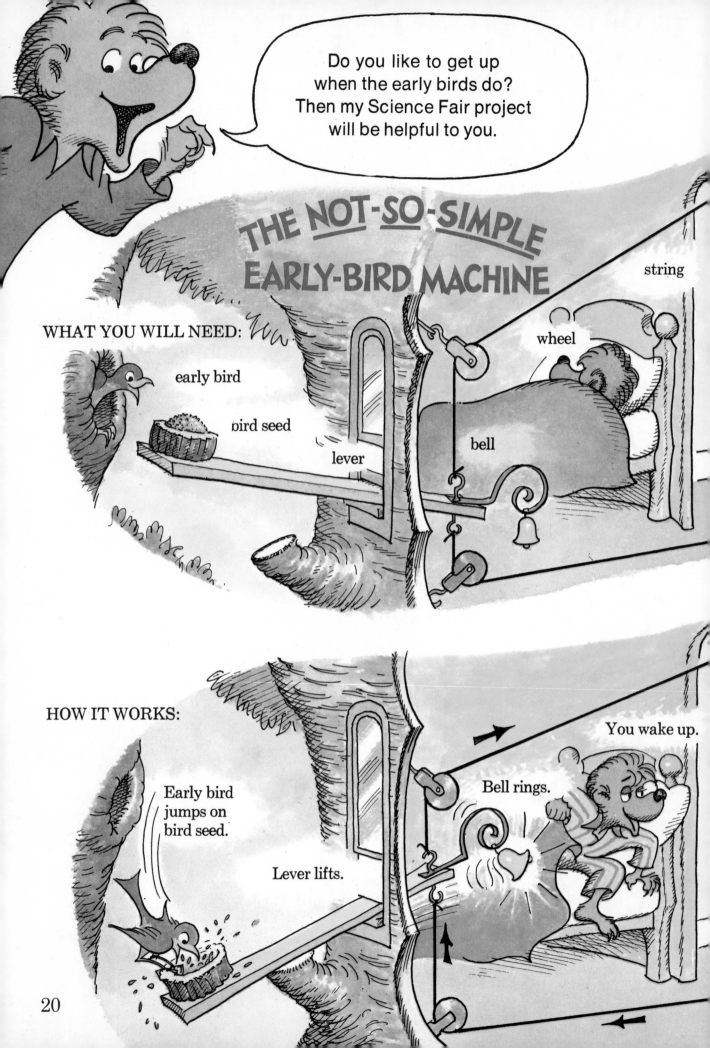

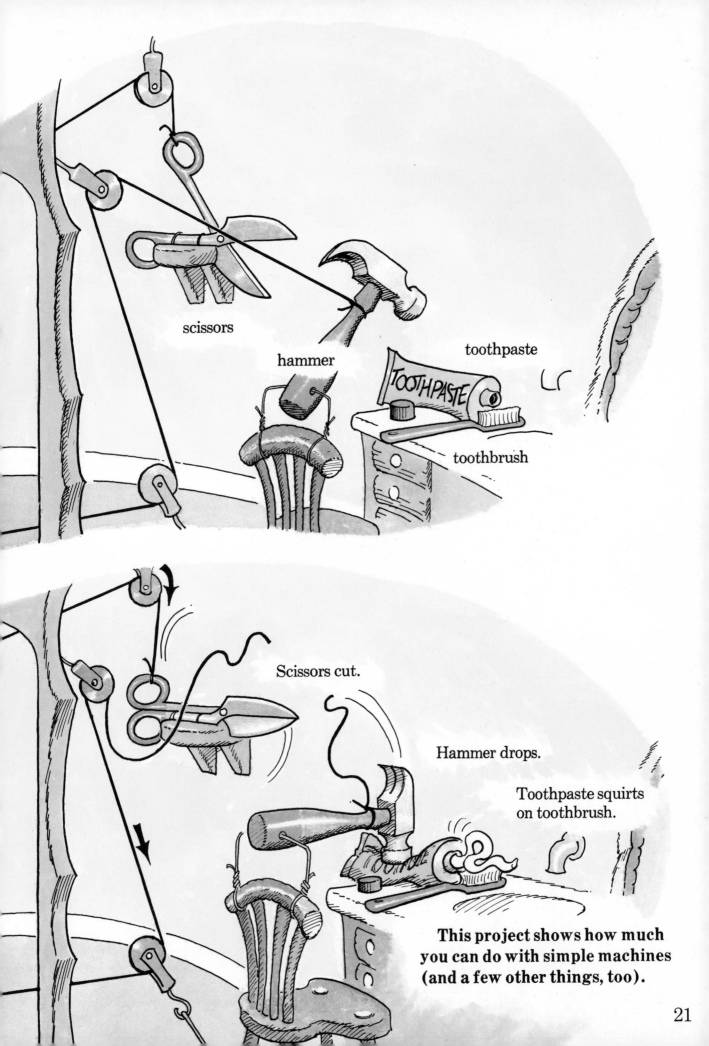

scissors

hammer

toothpaste

TOOTHPASTE

toothbrush

Scissors cut.

Hammer drops.

Toothpaste squirts
on toothbrush.

**This project shows how much
you can do with simple machines
(and a few other things, too).**

Thanks for the lessons,
Papa Bear!
Now we're all set
for the Science Fair.

Not so fast!
You're not ready yet.
There are more
science lessons
you have to get.

22

But, Papa! . . .
Look over there!
They're getting ready
for the Science Fair.

We have lots of time.
Just stop the chatter.
I still have to teach you
some facts about **matter**.

23

ACTUAL FACTS ABOUT MATTER

WHAT IS MATTER?

Anything that has weight and takes up room is matter.

There are many kinds of matter.

Some kinds are heavy. A small amount may weigh many pounds.

THE THREE KINDS OF MATTER

I still remember from my science class that matter can be **solid** or **liquid** or **gas**.

1. SOLID

A PIECE OF MATTER THAT KEEPS ITS SHAPE IS CALLED A SOLID.

There are <u>many</u> solids.
They're all around—
those rocks, that sign,
this road, the ground...

Now what other solids
do we see?

That tree! Papa Bear.
Look out for that tree!

27

BONK

Wow! That was some solid, that giant oak tree.

Yes. That was a solid. I do agree.

While Mom and Dad are making repairs, let's name some solids with the two little bears.

ACTUAL FACTUAL BEAR

HOW MANY SOLIDS CAN WE NAME?

Hmm...
Let's see.

wood

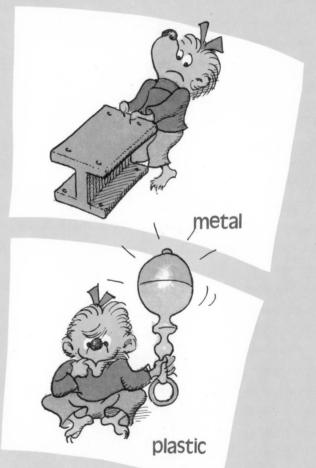

metal

glass

plastic

Rubber's a solid
that is elastic!

We're partly solids.

claw

tooth

muscle

bone

So is the earth.

sand

soil

clay

stone

We wear some solids.

straw

shell

cotton

feather

gold

wool

nylon

leather

30

Some solids we <u>eat</u>.

2. LIQUID

LIQUID IS MATTER THAT HAS NO SHAPE OF ITS OWN. IT FLOWS AND POURS.

Are we ready for liquids?
Ah! I see that you are.
Without liquids to drink,
we wouldn't get far.

The most useful liquid—
Are you listening, Daughter?
The most useful liquid . . .

33

... is the one we call WATER!

WATER AND HOW WE USE IT

FOR DRINKING
We use water from rivers and streams and underground wells.

FOR TRANSPORTATION
By using boats, we can travel wherever there is enough water.

FOR RAISING FOOD
Plants won't grow without it.

WATER WORKS

ACTUAL FACTUAL BEAR

34

FOR WASHING
We can't keep clean
without water.

FOR FIGHTING FIRES
Water can put out
most fires.

FIRE BOAT

FOR KEEPING COOL
A-a-a-ah!

MILL

FOR POWER
Water flowing downhill turns
waterwheels. This wheel
is turning a grindstone
that grinds wheat into flour.

35

The most useful liquid
is water, it's true.
But other liquids
are useful, too.

OTHER USEFUL LIQUIDS

GASOLINE makes motors go.

OIL makes them run smoothly.

DYE colors cloth.

ALCOHOL kills germs.

Some liquids are useful because
they harden into solids.

glue

nail polish

concrete

3. GAS

GAS IS MATTER THAT HAS NO SHAPE AT ALL. IT CAN BE COLLECTED IN A CLOSED CONTAINER, OR IT CAN SPREAD OUT IN THE AIR.

37

A gas balloon!
Lucky for us
we happened to pass!
This is our chance
to learn about gas.

But, Papa, that sign
makes it very clear.
There may be a chance
of some danger here!

Not for a gas
expert like me!
To understand gases,
use this as a key:

Solids and liquids take up
a limited space.
But gases spread out
all over the place.

There's helium gas
in this small tank.
Hmmm . . . I wonder
what happens
when you turn the crank.

The balloon goes up!
That's what happens, Pop.
And I do not think
it is going to stop!

Papa!
What makes it fly?
What makes the balloon
go up so high?

A very good question,
Sister Bear!
Helium gas
is lighter than air!

41

The THREE KINDS OF MATTER are what you will see when you do this science experiment with me.

1 Start with ice.

Ice is a SOLID. ———————

It has weight. It takes up space. And ice has a shape of its own.

2 Take ice from the freezer.

Let it melt.

3 It will all change to water.

Water is a LIQUID.

It still has weight.
It still takes up space...

but it no longer has a shape of its own.
It flows and pours.

42

4 Next, heat the water.

5 Let it boil.

6 It will all change to steam.

Steam is a GAS.

It still has weight.
It still takes up space.
But now it has no shape at all!

Now you know that matter can change its form when the temperature gets a little too warm.

Note: Not all solids are as easy to change as ice, but all solids—even rock—will change if they get hot enough.

43

THE THREE KINDS
OF MATTER:
SOLID, LIQUID
& GAS.

NOT-SO
EARLY-B...

...PLE
...RD MACHINE

LEVE...

Thank you, Papa.
Those lessons were fun.
We really appreciate
all you have done.

And thanks to your
lessons, Papa Bear,
we all have good projects
for the fair!

That's right, Small Bear,
the three of you do—
but I plan to make
a project, too.
So, hold everything now,
and wait for me!

You still have to learn about **energy**!

45

ACTUAL FACTS ABOUT ENERGY

WHAT IS ENERGY?

Energy is what it takes to get things done!

Any kind of work or play takes **ENERGY**, my son.

Energy is the "go" of things.
Without energy to make things happen,
there would be no movement or change.

SOURCES OF ENERGY

There's energy
in wind and water.
Fuel is another source.
But where do <u>we</u> get "go"?

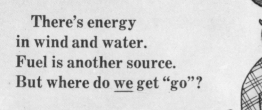

We get it from food,
of course.

THE BURGER BEAR

1. ENERGY FROM FOOD

OUR BODIES TURN
THE FOOD WE EAT
INTO THE ENERGY
WE NEED TO WORK
AND PLAY.

...lease.

...ble,

...Papa Bear

...ble!

THE BURGER

HOW OUR BODIES TURN FOOD INTO ENERGY

Teeth chew food into small pieces. It travels to
the stomach, where it is dissolved by stomach juices.

Dissolved food passes into the bloodstream.
It is now ready to be used as energy.

If we eat more than we need it is stored in the body as fat!

So I'm not overweight,
you see,
I just have too much
energy!

2. ENERGY FROM FUEL

THERE IS ENERGY IN MATTER. FUEL IS MATTER THAT IS BURNED TO GET ENERGY.

Wow!
There's sure a lot of "go"
going on down there!

And almost all of it
comes from fuel, Small Bear.

NATURAL GAS STORAGE

JET FUEL

49

ACTUAL FACTS ABOUT
ENERGY
WHAT IS ENERGY?

Energy is what it takes
to get things done!

Any kind of work or play
takes **ENERGY**, my son.

Energy is the "go" of things.
Without energy to make things happen,
there would be no movement or change.

SOURCES OF ENERGY

There's energy
in wind and water.
Fuel is another source.
But where do _we_ get "go"?

We get it from food,
of course.

THE BURGER BEAR

1. ENERGY FROM FOOD

OUR BODIES TURN
THE FOOD WE EAT
INTO THE ENERGY
WE NEED TO WORK
AND PLAY.

THE BURGER

Four burgers, please.
And if it isn't
too much trouble,
make mine a Papa Bear
super-double!

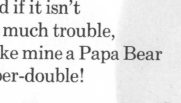

HOW OUR BODIES TURN FOOD INTO ENERGY

Teeth chew food into small pieces. It travels to
the stomach, where it is dissolved by stomach juices.

Dissolved food passes into the bloodstream.

It is now ready to be used as energy.

If we eat more than we need it is stored in the body as fat!

So I'm not overweight,
you see,
I just have too much
energy!

THE BURGER BEAR

2. ENERGY FROM FUEL

THERE IS ENERGY IN MATTER. FUEL IS MATTER THAT IS BURNED TO GET ENERGY.

Wow!
There's sure a lot of "go" going on down there!

And almost all of it comes from fuel, Small Bear.

NATURAL GAS STORAGE

JET FUEL

The most important fuels are oil, coal and natural gas. They were made in the earth millions of years ago.

It takes a long time for the earth to make fuels—a lot longer than it takes us to use them up. So be careful not to waste them.

ENERGY FROM
3. WIND and WATER

MOVING AIR AND MOVING WATER CAN GIVE US USEFUL ENERGY.

Wind is moving air.
It can be very strong.
It can push a sailboat
right along.

That is very
interesting, Pop.
But it's pushing this sailboat
toward quite a drop!

52

Well, don't just stand
around and look!
Help me with
this grappling hook.

HOW WE USE WATER
TO MAKE ELECTRICITY

A wall is built
across a swift stream.

It is called a dam.

Water builds up
behind the dam.
Some of it is
allowed to spill over.

This falling water turns
waterwheels that run special
machines called generators.
These change the energy
of the falling water into
electrical energy.

This electrical energy
comes to us over wires.

53

Electrical energy can help us do all these jobs— and a few more, too.

heating

cooling

washing

drying

lighting

roasting

toasting

frying

54

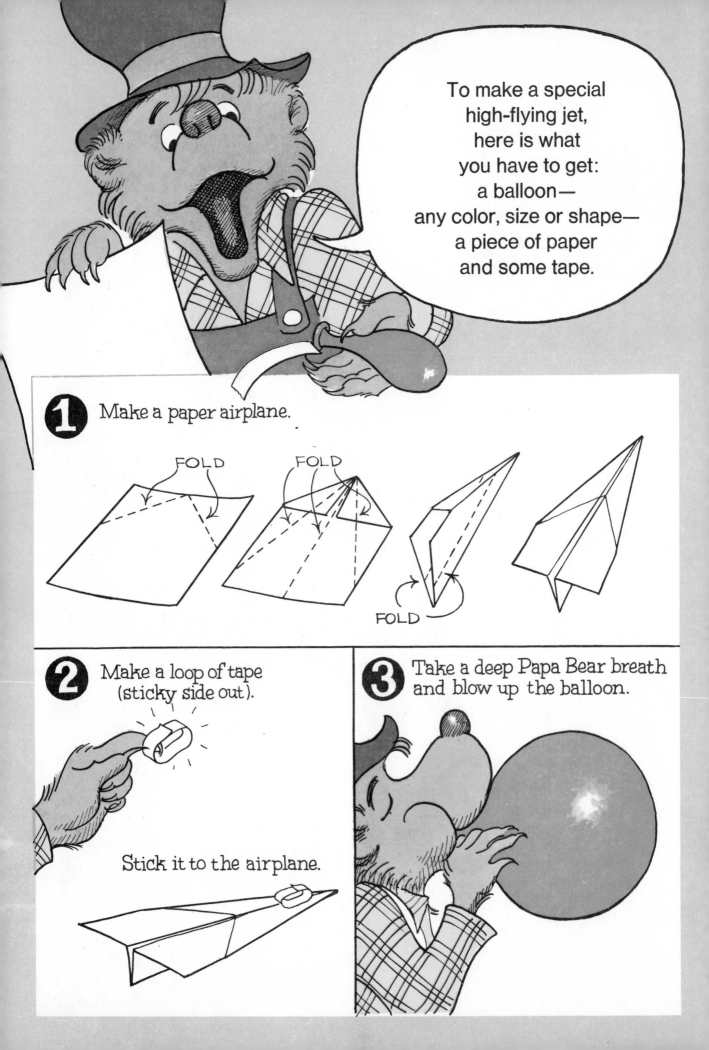

To make a special
high-flying jet,
here is what
you have to get:
a balloon—
any color, size or shape—
a piece of paper
and some tape.

1 Make a paper airplane.

FOLD   FOLD

FOLD

2 Make a loop of tape (sticky side out).

Stick it to the airplane.

3 Take a deep Papa Bear breath and blow up the balloon.

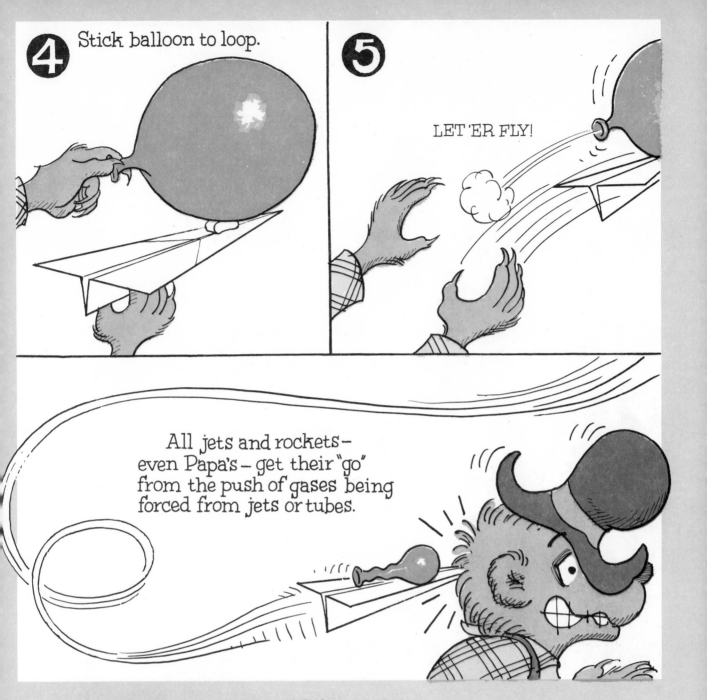

4 Stick balloon to loop.

5 LET 'ER FLY!

All jets and rockets—
even Papa's—get their "go"
from the push of gases being
forced from jets or tubes.

**It's fun to experiment with jet power.
Here are some more high-fliers.**

twin engine

moon shot

blimp

Now we all
have projects
to show.
Come, Papa Bear.
Let us go!

We really love
your lessons, Pop.
But isn't it time
for them to—

58

STOP!

No more time for talk,
Small Bear!
They're about to start . . .

59

...THE SCIENCE FAIR!

At last! . . . And as soon as the Bear Family sets up its projects, The Bears' Science Fair will be officially open.